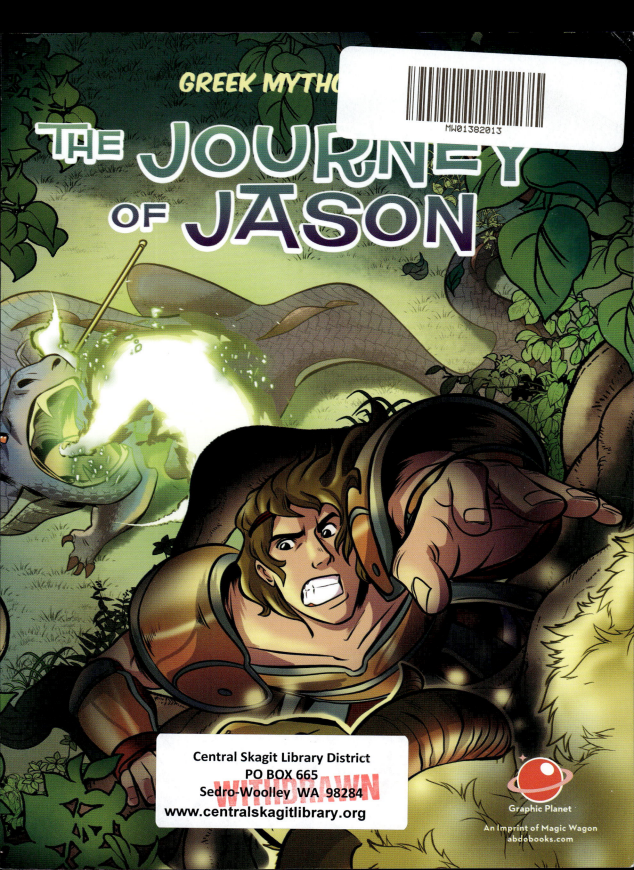

THIS BOOK IS DEDICATED TO ALL THE TEACHERS WHO STRIVE TO GUIDE AND TO INSTRUCT, PREPARING STUDENTS FOR THEIR OWN ADVENTURES OF A LIFETIME. –DC

TO EVERYONE WHO LOVES A GREAT GREEK STORY ESPECIALLY MY CAT MIMITO. ILLUSTRATING THIS COLLECTION WAS CHALLENGING AND FUN. I LOVED THE WHOLE PROCESS. –LA

abdobooks.com

Published by Magic Wagon, a division of ABDO, PO Box 398166, Minneapolis, Minnesota 55439. Copyright © 2022 by Abdo Consulting Group, Inc. International copyrights reserved in all countries. No part of this book may be reproduced in any form without written permission from the publisher. Graphic Planet™ is a trademark and logo of Magic Wagon.

Printed in the United States of America, North Mankato, Minnesota.
102021
012022

Written by David Campiti
Illustrated and Colored by Lelo Alves
Lettered by Kathryn S. Renta
Editorial Supervision by David Campiti/MJ Macedo
Packaged by Glass House Graphics
Research Assistance by Matt Simmons
Art Directed by Candice Keimig
Editorial Support by Tamara L. Britton

Library of Congress Control Number: 2021941252

Publisher's Cataloging-in-Publication Data

Names: Campiti, David, author. | Alves, Lelo, illustrator.
Title: The journey of Jason / by David Campiti ; illustrated by Lelo Alves.
Description: Minneapolis, Minnesota : Magic Wagon, 2022. | Series: Greek mythology
Summary: Jason seeks the Golden Fleece in a graphic novel interpretation of this classic Greek myth.
Identifiers: ISBN 9781098231804 (lib. bdg.) | ISBN 9781644946626 (pbk.) | ISBN 9781098232368 (ebook) | ISBN 9781098232641 (Read-to-Me ebook)
Subjects: LCSH: Jason (Mythological character)--Juvenile fiction. | Mythology, Greek--Juvenile fiction. | Gods, Greek--Juvenile fiction. | Heroes--Juvenile fiction. | Adventure stories--Juvenile fiction. | Graphic Novels--Juvenile fiction.
Classification: DDC 741.5--dc23

TABLE OF CONTENTS

CHARACTER GUIDE 4

THE JOURNEY OF JASON 5

WHAT DO YOU THINK? 30

MYSTERIES BEHIND THE MYTHS 31

GLOSSARY & ONLINE RESOURCES 32

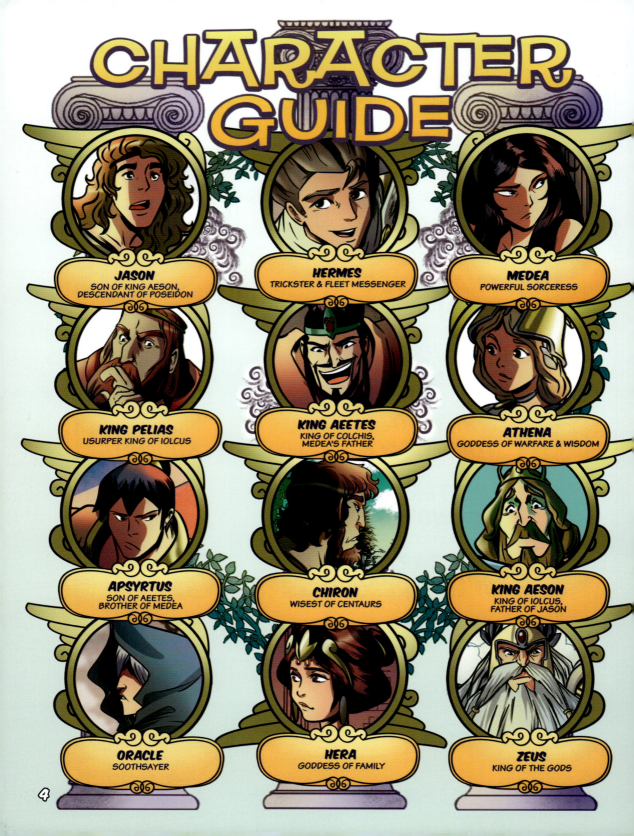

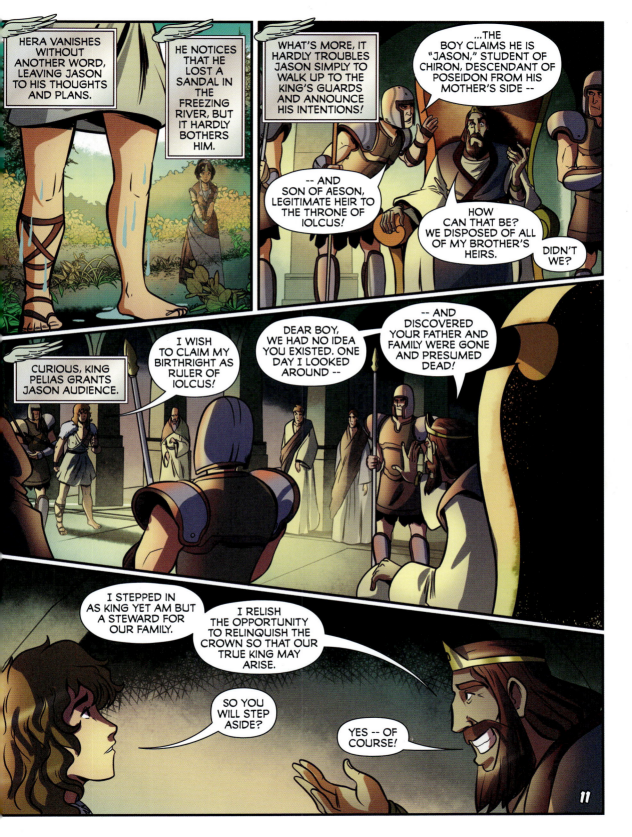

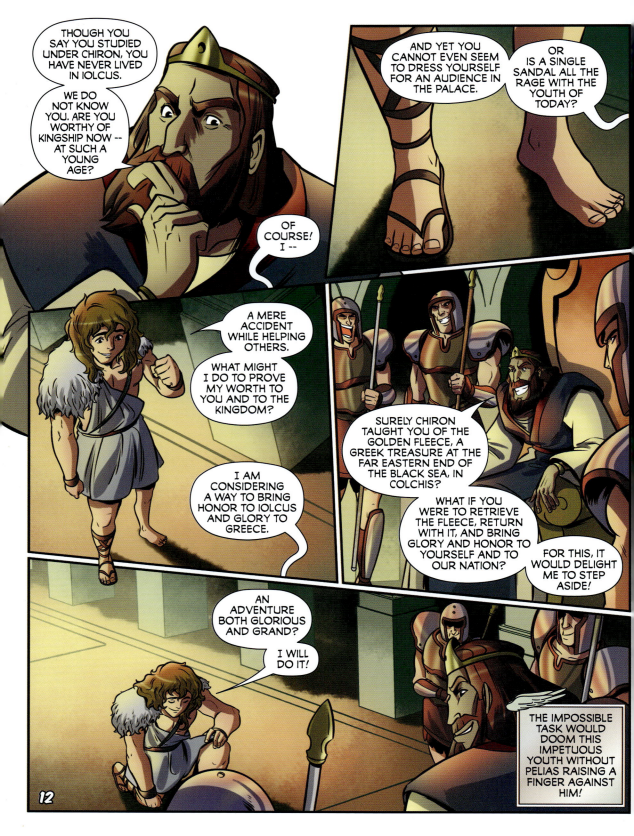

WHAT DO YOU THINK?

1. Jason is a flawed hero, because no man or woman is perfect. Although he did great things amid grand adventures, he left Medea for a younger princess on the promise of ruling a kingdom when his own birthright was denied. What might you learn from his behaviors and decisions?

2. Medea was a powerful sorceress descended from the bloodline of Circe. Her undying love for Jason was god-given, forced upon her by Eros so that she would aid Jason in his quest for the Golden Fleece. When Jason chose to leave her, that love was something she could not restrain. Was Medea alone responsible for her own actions? Why or why not?

3. What responsibility, if any, should Eros take for the fatal consequences of Medea's actions? What about Hera or Athena, who directed Eros to imbue Medea with such intense, eternal love? Should each person take responsibility for the consequences of his or her own actions? Why or why not?

4. Myths lived vibrant in the lives of the Greeks, because the stories occurred in familiar locations. Mount Olympus is Greece's highest mountain. Iolcus is now the port city of Volos. Corinth is a city on the Peloponnese peninsula. When you first read Greek mythology, did you know that these were real places?

5. In parts of Greece, a sheep's fleece was stretched over wooden frames and placed into streams. Flecks of gold collected in it from nearby deposits. The fleece was hung to dry before the gold was brushed out. Do you think this is how the myth of a Golden Fleece came about?

MYSTERIES BEHIND THE MYTHS

1. A master shipbuilder named Argus led design and construction of the great ship named the *Argo*; some myths suggest the goddess Athena gave inspiration to this, the first ship of its kind built specifically for high seas voyages.

2. Jason and the Argonauts encounter many other adventures while on their quest for the Golden Fleece, tales not chronicled in this book. It says much for Jason's character that Heracles was a crewman, not captain, of such a hearty band of heroes.

3. Several myths about Medea tell of different fates for her after she takes revenge on Jason for breaking his vow. In one, Medea escapes to Thebes, a city in central Greece. There, she finds and heals Heracles from a curse Hera put on him. He gives Medea a place to stay in Thebes until angry Thebans drive her away.

4. In another myth, Medea flees to Athens, where she meets and marries Aegeus. They have a son together. When Aegeus's long-lost son Theseus returns, Medea tells Aegeus that Theseus is a phony and a threat. She attempts to poison Theseus, but Aegeus recognizes the sword Theseus carries as his own. He knocks the poison from Medea's hand and saves his son.

5. The winged ram Chrysomallos grew golden wool and became a Greek symbol of authority and kingship. The ram was the offspring of Poseidon (in a primitive ram-form) and Theophane, granddaughter of sun god Helios. Helios was Medea's grandfather.

GLOSSARY

AEETES — Savage king of Colchis who possesses the Golden Fleece.

ARGO — Large 50-oared ship sailed by The Argonauts.

ARGONAUTS — The heroes whom Jason gathered for his grand quest aboard the Argo. They included Acastus, Admetus, Argus (chief builder of the Argo), Atalanta, Augeas, the Boreads Zetes and Calais, the Dioscuri Castor & Polydeukes, Euphemus, Eurytus, Heracles, Idas, Idmon, Lynceus, Meleager, Orpheus, Peleus, Telamon, and Tiphys.

CHIRON — Wisest and most just of all the centaurs, a teacher to several gods and heroes in their youth.

CIRCE — Powerful sorceress and aunt to Medea.

COLCHIS — A kingdom on the Black Sea.

GREECE — A mountainous country with many islands, located on the Mediterranean Sea. Considered the birthplace of democracy and early mathematical and scientific principles and the place from which the gods ruled.

HERA — Goddess of childbirth, family, marriage, and women.

HERMES — The divine trickster, son of Zeus and Maia, he is the emissary and fleet messenger of the gods. He even conducted souls into the afterlife.

IOLCUS — The lands to which Jason was heir to the throne. Zeus's wife.

JASON — Son of Aeson and Alcimede, rightful king and queen of Iolcus, and great-grandson to Hermes, the messenger god.

MEDEA — Powerful sorceress. Direct descendant of Helios, niece to the sorceress Circe. Daughter of King Aeetes and the Oceanid Idyia.

MOUNT OLYMPUS — A real mountain in Thessaly, Greece, towering nearly 9,800 feet (2,987 m) above the sea. This is the site around which the mythology for the gods was created.

OLYMPIA — The fabled city that the gods inhabited and from which Zeus ruled, located at the top of Mount Olympus.

ORACLE — A priestess who interprets various signs to foretell the future.

PELIAS — Half-brother of Jason's father Aeson. He murdered Jason's family to become king.

ZEUS — God of lightning, son of Cronus and Rhea, husband to Hera, he fought a great and terrible war to become king of the gods of Olympus.

ONLINE RESOURCES

To learn more about **GREEK MYTHOLOGY**, visit abdobooklinks.com or scan this QR code. These links are routinely monitored and updated to provide the most current information available.